180 Degrees of Subconscious Intuitions Around

The Ocean & Moon:

Feminine Frequencies

Tyrone Dicks

www.IVPTME.com

This Double Book is Dedicated to

Katherine E. Dicks

A Strong Foundation Makes The Difference.

180 Degrees Of Subconscious Intuitions Around The Ocean & Moon: Feminine Frequencies© 2024 by, *Tyrone Dicks,* an Imprint of Innovative View-Point

The content contained within this book may not be reproduced, duplicated or transmitted without direct permission by the Author or the Publisher.

Under no circumstances with the blame of any legal responsibility be held against the publisher, or author for any damages, or reparations, or monetary loss due to the information that's within this book. Either directly or indirectly. You are responsible for your own choices, actions and results.

Legal Notice:

This book is copyright protected. This book is only for personal use. You cannot amend, distribute, sell, use, quote, or sell any part, or the content within this book, without the consent of the author or publisher.

Disclaimer Notice:

Please note the information that's contained within this document is for educational and entertainment purposes only. All efforts have been executed to present accurate, up to date, reliable, and complete information. No warranties of any kind are declared or implied. Readers acknowledge that the author is not engaging in the rendering of legal, financial, medical or professional advice. The content within this book has derived from various sources. Please consult a licensed professional before attempting any techniques outlined in this book.

By reading this document, the reader agrees and understands that under no circumstance is the author responsible for any losses, direct or indirect, which are incurred as a result of the use of the information contained within this document, including but not limiting to, - errors, omissions or inaccuracies.

For more information, or to book an event, contact:

Admin@IVPTME.com

www.IVPTME.com

Book design by Tyrone Dicks

Cover design by Tyrone Dicks

ISBN   - Paperback: 979-8-9902851-0-1

LCCN - Paperback: 2024906906

Special Thanks

Shanika Black
Taysia Epperson
Laura Taylor
Zenobia Brown
Melissa Rice

Focusing on *Deep Breathing* and *Concentration* of Imagination while *Meditating, can* open your Chakras. Think wise.

You Are A Super Hero. Tap Into Your Potential.

CONTENTS

1. INSPIRATION-----------------------------------3
2. PATRIOTISM------------------------------------27
3. SPIRITUAL-------------------------------------47
4. DISTRESS--------------------------------------69
5. EITHER--117
ABOUT THE AUTHOR-------------------------------193
ACKNOWLEDGMENTS--------------------------------195

180 Degrees Of Subconscious Intuitions Around The Ocean & Moon: Feminine Frequencies

Introduction

First and Foremost, I want to Thank You for letting this Book touch another reader/author's hands, and for taking it off the crowded book store shelf. This creative work of art is an Inspirational Road-Map in the direction of elevating your frequencies and vibrating on a higher level

The masterpiece before you, are an assortment of my past experiences, interactions, reflections of emotions, opinions of instances, interpretations on how I would react in differing scenarios.

You may or may not, thoroughly enjoy these compositions of poetic literature that's compiled within this brief synopsis of my thought's abroad.

Be aware, yet-*inspired* by my mindset and critical thinking. Let my instances be examples. Navigate through this life we live, knowing more than what you knew before opening this book and broadening your paradigm on a new note. To thinking outside-of-the-box.

Show pride and be a *Patriot* for what you stand for and love. Never let anyone sway your thinking, especially if it goes against your integrity, beliefs, mantra, loved ones and your Spirit.

Let yourself be open to the possibilities of everything that has the *essence of Spirit*. Meditating, opening your Chakras, channeling energy flow: are all beneficial when understanding what you truly capable of. We are the Super Hero's & Villains of Saturday a.m. cartoons of the 80's & 90's. The Faith of a mustard seed.

I've been down… but, I got back up. Plenty of times and over the same scenarios at most. I was a glutton to failure for most of my life; in conjunction of following someone's direction towards failure. A beautiful goddess once said, 'If at first you don't succeed… try and try again'. At times, it takes game changer, trend-setter to go through the toughest times of their lives; because fire molds coal to diamonds, from the ruff.
Before obtaining great position, you must follow and know failure innately; This Alone Breeds Great Leaders.

Feeling luxurious lately? Unwind with a little *euphoria* for your system. Just don't over indulge. I STRONGLY advise that you take portions of Me in moderation. Too much of anything isn't good for the soul. *Be advised, that the content within Utopia is suitable for the mature crowd only*. With that said, have fun, let your mind run ramp-id on endless possibilities and perception of instances.

Tyrone Dicks

Hopefully, this *Book* of 90 Poems can aide as a steppingstone to self-awareness, inner-attainment and inspire you to obtaining everything to your heart's potential and content.

180 Degrees Of Subconscious Intuitions Around The Ocean & Moon: Feminine Frequencies

"Inspiration"

A 'Spark' of Optimism fueled by internal strength and loved ones.

Tyrone Dicks

180 Degrees Of Subconscious Intuitions Around The Ocean & Moon: Feminine Frequencies

"In-cognitive Power"

Lately I've been having premonitions.
Wishing my sentiments into existence.
As recent events have urged my persistence.
To manifest my dreams with extreme prejudice.

Because independence results from commitments.
A will to win with a standby contingence.
Relentless being content from the hearts of men and women.
Contending for control with a hint of arrogance.

As an allegiance is formed to prevent them from being extinguished.
With a lenience on racial essence and background etiquette.
Some speak so eloquently, articulately but with a hit of ratchetness an Ebonics.
Yet they're all decent pieces to the puzzle that flow in sequence.

They are adamant, intensive, extensive and some might be a friend.
With intricate beliefs and comprehension dialogues but it's their prerogative.
Above all be inspired, as we all have one life to live.
What lies ahead can make us or break us, just know, there's power in thoughts, as it's in-cognitive.

Tyrone Dicks

180 Degrees Of Subconscious Intuitions Around The Ocean & Moon: Feminine Frequencies

"Just Chill"

Just chill... Try to breathe, relax and make amends.
If all fails, count to ten and back down again.
A lot could change if we all had that one friend.
That we can count on, that one whom we could truly depend.

They tell us what we need to know versus what we want to hear.
They barely sugarcoat things, they'll give it to us raw and uncut, without fear.
They're the ones who gain our unconditional gratitude and whom we don't see the most.
But crossing the line of lust and friendship could mean you're making them disappear.

So, smile and make today your bitch and tomorrow your opposition.
For the one you need to vent to is at your fingertips or the tip of your intuition.
Position yourself in life according to where you will need to be with no one's permission.
To act the way, you are without people acting bi-polar towards you, trying to revise your intentions.

If all fails just chill, try to breathe and ignore everyone's stares.
Let the world be your oyster and have sweet dreams with a hint of beautiful nightmares.
Or get on the phone and don't try to make them your own.
But contact that one you don't really know, but you know-that truly cares.

Tyrone Dicks

180 Degrees Of Subconscious Intuitions Around The Ocean & Moon: Feminine Frequencies

"Independent Fireworks"

I've been looking for love in all the wrong places.
As they were lessons learned in life where I struggled in different phases.

Romance, family, friendships, work and parental; from all, I had to resort back to the basics.
To gather myself in harmony and to feel each instance on a karmic basis.
Now knowing the world is one big platform and I choked on a lot of surreal stages.
The impact of embarrassment was potent, feelings; I was being gawked at by humility-naked.

Seeing the faces of many races, felt like I was being charged with a few cases.
As onlookers gawked in awe because they're energy was corrupt and contagious.
Nevertheless, I stood correct in my book of life as I flipped through the pages.
Of a new chapter, awakening my dormant character, for an open book test; and I aced it.

Not in this or the next lifetime, will I give into failure, no matter what's the wages.
I will always prevail and shine, I have a sublime mind and residual spiritual traces.
With little to no help, as I owe it to my higher powers and myself, for everything that I'm worth.
Humble in my ways as I give all to thee with divine praise; my Independent Fireworks.

Tyrone Dicks

180 Degrees Of Subconscious Intuitions Around The Ocean & Moon: Feminine Frequencies

"Honest intentions"

Be honest with honest intentions.
No matter whomever you may encounter.
If they respond with dishonest commitments.
Then they will show you-you're not whom they're fond of.

Disestablish yourself from fakes and liars.
Especially, if they start acting weird towards you.
Beware of what you seek and watch what you say.
Because there's no telling of what they may do.

They may cause you disdain, feelings or resentment to finish a task.
That of what you may not profit nor gain.
Although, you may gain some anxiety from the farce.
From what they say, as they've experienced a whole lot of pain.

Be careful of what you wish for, and hope that you get more...
From impostors that thrive on your submission.
If you're ever in doubt, just breathe and pick one from a crowd.
That you think have honest intentions.

Tyrone Dicks

180 Degrees Of Subconscious Intuitions Around The Ocean & Moon: Feminine Frequencies

Discipline: To Endure"

Duration could be contentment in a timely manner.
Pending if you see the cup as half empty or half full.
They say patience is a virtue or could it be finances.
To each is own, but you would see better if you remove the wool.

Few struggle within a day, with their own thoughts.
Some struggle within a year concerning their crafts.
Or vice versa but, most have struggled all their life, just to have sacrificed.
Above all, some struggle could be avoided if you learn to laugh.

Your trash could be someone's treasure as the saying goes.
And what I love, could be your lust, for but a moment.
No matter of how we view our different scenarios.
Take pride or joy in it, or whatever, just own it.

Tyrone Dicks

180 Degrees Of Subconscious Intuitions Around The Ocean & Moon: Feminine Frequencies

"Obtainable Heights"

The fight was real.
My life was strife.
Nobody will stop me.
From obtainable heights.

Some friends and family crossed me.
And I can show the proof.
I brushed my shoulders off and struggled.
If you were me, what would you do.

True Facts: Nobody gave me shit.
I showed love and paid with Interest!
Most handouts were counterfeit.
I gave advancements but it was nonexistent.

Only a few can say they helped me.
In this life; I've paved my way.
Not counting on anyone, I got my back.
Achieving all of my goals, sponsored by my faith.

Forever loving my Higher Powers.
They also helped me from the hole I dug.
Although they punish me like my parents.
No matter the penalty I'll struggle to show much love.

My actions matured and pure.
My intent is to keep it thorough.
I live my life with honor.
If I fuck with you, I'm forever loyal.

From my past, I learned the game.
And how to maintain my emotions abroad.

Tyrone Dicks

No father, or uncles to teach me.
And when I failed, I recovered from my own downfalls.

I molded myself from failures.
I built my mantra all throughout my actions.
I'm sculpting myself from the chi and of my ancestors.
Soon to be blessed, I'm ready, wuz hah'nen.

A lonely road I'm prepared to walk.
Not to mention the one I left behind.
New pains is expected and may await me.
As Failures not an Option, defines my Grind.

I brush off the stares that's irrelevant.
And soak in some mockery that's congruent.
I may smile or even joke with your sentiments.
I have thick skin and I'm not easily influenced.

Emotions intact so nothing won't hit home.
Yet, the pride of a bull, and I covered all bases.
Too late to try and stop me from Obtainable Heights.
Look Mom I did it, I Officially finally made it.

180 Degrees Of Subconscious Intuitions Around The Ocean & Moon: Feminine Frequencies

"Growth Spurt"

Let no-one damper your mood, keep your energy high, that's law.
Even if someone rain on your parade stay cool.
Don't go on a tirade, instead just brush it off.
Indeed, they'll piss you off, just use it as gas-your fuel.

Focus... It can throw you off your course.
A projected path to all of your dreams and goals.
I know it to be true, consequences as a real witness.
My anger, that frequency has put my aspirations on hold.

A word from the wise, disguise your pride.
And keep your feelings on one accord.
They'll attack your emotions, if they know they can control them.
So, all their looks and mockery stay cool and ignore.

They'll try to degrade you, pay attention for what I say is true.
They may drag your name all through the dirt.
They might inflict so much pain, regardless don't be ashamed.
If you don't concentrate and redirect it, you'll be awaiting an inevitable growth spurt.

Tyrone Dicks

180 Degrees Of Subconscious Intuitions Around The Ocean & Moon: Feminine Frequencies

"Much Love"

Spread joy and love and let it radiate.
Be magnetic and let it exude through your pours.
Brush off negativity and don't let doubt penetrate.
Be self-sustaining, and let your mind be an open door.

We need new creators in this world of monotony.
Dare to be different, your unique let it show.
Don't be trendy, be a trendsetter to begin with.
Unravel your mind, don't be consumed, let it explode.

With ideas that's poetic or contemporary.
Some fashions, innovations and abroad.
A path of greatness could be yours in the making.
Don't talk yourself out of it, thinking your flawed, it'll be your loss.

Take Pride in your work, but not too much of it.
If you are not motivated, be inspired by my interpretations.
Anything is possible if you think it, you surely can achieve it.
Talk it into existence, with much love and action, and try not to worry; have patience.

Tyrone Dicks

180 Degrees Of Subconscious Intuitions Around The Ocean & Moon: Feminine Frequencies

"Parked-N-Spaces"

Sometimes, I have to get away, to gather my thoughts.
Sometimes, I have to brush off the what if's, and what nots.
Sometimes, not being myself saves me from my own faults.
Because, if I react to their actions, it'll be at a cost.

The ones we love.
Knows what arguments to pursue.
Like clockwork, they know what buttons to push.
How we tick and how we move.

Just to get the response they want.
It's like they have a point to prove.
In the end, it would all be worthless.
Because we all have a lot, we can lose.

Just get up and go, no matter where, you may roam.
Just get up and go, where there's silence and no phones.
Just get up and go, to the empty parking lots, to be left all alone.

Just get up and go, even if you have to call another place home.

If someone can make you angry.
No matter what they may do.
You will have given all of your power to them.
And you will be so easy to bruise.

The same goes for all for all chemistry.
Within both a physical and emotional response.
Rather it be lust, hurt or envy.
They'll know your energy and what it wants.

Tyrone Dicks

So, if you're ever overwhelmed with pressure, when loves vacant.
From your spouse, family member, a friend or even other races.
Just get up and go, make no mistakes just embrace it.
Then vent it all out and breathe, while parked-N-spaces.

180 Degrees Of Subconscious Intuitions Around The Ocean & Moon: Feminine Frequencies

"To Live Again"

I know I had my share of round and round carousels.
Ups and downs made me stronger, though, I know they cannot tell.
Tribulations of the trials lived, gone through; broke me down right to my core.
I picked my face off grounds because my purpose I won't ignore.

The more and more I go though, I feel I have a point to prove.
All day I strive to show you, my ways won't be brand new.
You know my style, it's all love, envy would be just my luck.
My essences say, whom I do it for... and it's all because ...

I want to live again.
My love is close to perfect...
I want to live again.
Hard to trust somebody because so many has hurt méh...

I want to live again.
Unite me with my better half you know I'm worthy...
I want to live again.
My love, my life, my friend, to live again.

Tyrone Dicks

180 Degrees Of Subconscious Intuitions Around The Ocean & Moon: Feminine Frequencies

"No Matter What"

You will never win.
If you never try.
As failure is not an option.
Just don't succumb to your pride.

Just give it all you got.
And don't give up, no matter what.
You can't finish if you never start.
Remember, you'll get no glory if you have no guts.

The moral of the story is...
Never let anyone tell you what you can or cannot do.
You only owe it to yourself.
When it's concerning a point to prove.

Be inspired... Go the length... You can move mountains.
You can do anything you set your mind too.
Standards are the bare minimum of what you know you can accomplish.
Set your goal a little higher when you've proven yourself wrong of what you thought you cannot do.

And once you're satisfied with where your bar or goal is...
You can keep it there for however long you want because...
You've already proven yourself extraordinary again and again.
That you can do more than what you think you're capable of.

Don't give up... No Matter What.

Tyrone Dicks

180 Degrees Of Subconscious Intuitions Around The Ocean & Moon: Feminine Frequencies

"Patriotism"

Abstaining in Pride with a sense of Love for one's Community or Country.

Tyrone Dicks

180 Degrees Of Subconscious Intuitions Around The Ocean & Moon: Feminine Frequencies

"Battalions & Platoons"

Regardless of your branch or your division we are one.
Concerning battalions and platoons.
We have fought, we have bled, we have died for change.
Most importantly, we will be coming home soon.

We rally when it comes to making a difference.
No matter if it's foreign or domestic revolving places.
We don't take sides, unless logic's the motivator.
As were neutral, if there's a problem between races.

Were underway if our lively hood is threatened.
On ships, or fighter planes, or ground convoys.
Applying the pressure, not backing down for anyone.
We will seek, we will find, we will destroy.

Regardless of your branch or your division, we are one.
Conserving battalion and platoons.
We have fought, we have bled, we have died for change.
Mostly importantly, we will be coming home soon.

Tyrone Dicks

180 Degrees Of Subconscious Intuitions Around The Ocean & Moon: Feminine Frequencies

"Informal Uniforms"

No matter your dress code, or how you identify.
We all have an important role or responsibility.
Some may be more important, but for you all we rely.
So, don't take a stance of arrogance or humility.

We all may not be equal, but our ambition may be equivalent.
Our upbringing plays a big part, from then hence we were born.
Regardless if you're high or low in the chain of command among-st us all.
Were held reliable when we dawn our formal or informal uniforms.

Tyrone Dicks

180 Degrees Of Subconscious Intuitions Around The Ocean & Moon: Feminine Frequencies

"On The Watch"

On quarterdecks, I stand at attention.

I salute with a ratchet in hand.
I'm cool, although I'm intensive.

If you try to overtake my land.

On go, like green lights, and ain't waiting for it.
If you ever trespass or siege.

My home, my country and if you want war.
There are 50 million tactical soldiers better than me.

Over 3,000 gunships at the ready.

Over 10,000 armored Rhino's on Standby.
We got them thangs that'll turn you into Confetti.

We protect our own for honor, and for life.

So, if you ever think you wanna slide upon us.

Reconsider because no one else can do it better.
You're better off fighting off and entity or the corona.

For a war with us would be a lot of unwanted pressure.

Tyrone Dicks

180 Degrees Of Subconscious Intuitions Around The Ocean & Moon: Feminine Frequencies

"Patriarch's Protocol"

I man my post, securing the boats and ships ashore at port. Hoorah!
On base, we drill, severe at the pier, this isn't a lavish resort. Hoorah!

Deck hands, all crew, brigades, platoons, and everyone at the shipyard. Hoorah!
We prep, we train, we do everything to maintain, there's nothing we won't restrain. Hoorah!

For that day will come, one rise of the sun, air-crafts and drones alike. Hoorah!
Carriers and cruisers, destroyers and frigates, we'll plan, disperse, we'll fight. Hoorah!

We will stand and brawl and leave them in awe as some of us even may fall. Hoorah!
But within our walls of armor and honor, we'll never retreat or withdraw. Hoorah!

Our readiness demonstrates, we make no mistakes, were focused with attention to detail. Hoorah!
To find out their weakness, to eradicate with completion, will strive persistence and prevail. Hoorah!

Tyrone Dicks

180 Degrees Of Subconscious Intuitions Around The Ocean & Moon: Feminine Frequencies

"Enlistment"

Enlistments around the corner.
I'm nervous but never scared.
My adrenaline wants to jump on something.
I'm focused and stay prepared.

I hear about countless ports overseas.
Within 72 hrs. I'll be underway.
I hope I'm on a Destroyer or Carrier.
Being first amongst "A schools" hoping I will get my way.

They say I drink and curse like a squid.
And that I'm not lazy like a button pusher.
Sometimes I'm ready for whatever like lima beans.
And call shots often at times like Ice chippers.

Although my enlistment is around the corner.
I am nervous but never scared.
My adrenaline wants to jump on something.
I'm focused, and I try to stay prepared.

Tyrone Dicks

180 Degrees Of Subconscious Intuitions Around The Ocean & Moon: Feminine Frequencies

"A Wild Winning Streak"

Incentives are few but I'm up for promotion.
I can't wait until they unveil my upgrade.
Dedication speaks volumes, I'm fully devoted.
They know all of my effort and the zealous I gave.

I was fearless and proud; I went extra miles.
To obtain objectives on reconnaissance.
Just to show what I'm made of I went thought the mud.
To receive recognition and their promises.

I thought of some medals, a desk position and a raise.
Just to stay close to my family.
But I would go overseas in a minute notice to relieve.
All my comrades take heed of the man in me.

A wild winning streak is how I wanted my tour.
Looking back on it, in remembrance it was mostly fun.
Now I'm traveling back home, a familiar place where I roam.
Reporting for duty with my friends and all of my loved ones.

Tyrone Dicks

180 Degrees Of Subconscious Intuitions Around The Ocean & Moon: Feminine Frequencies

"Cadence

March to the tone my cadence.
My warfare is highly irregular.
I bully the bullies so flagrant.
It acts as my extra-curricular.

March to the tone of my cadence.
I call out to all outcasts unite!
All the homeless without families and vagrants.
We won't settle for less, we will fight!

March to the tone of my cadence.
I won't let adversaries get the best of me.
I'm not triggered by threats or their statements.
As I'm always on point, is my pedigree.

March to the tone of my cadence.
I grow wiser the older I get.
If I'm cornered, I resort to the basics.
I commit to my training and persist.

March to the tone of my cadence.
Myself is whom I depend.
I may forget some names but never the faces.
If you're for me, stick with me till the end.

Tyrone Dicks

180 Degrees Of Subconscious Intuitions Around The Ocean & Moon: Feminine Frequencies

"Boot Camp"

I'm tired of saluting at attention in ranks.
I'm tired of waking at 3 just to run.
I'm tired of 10–12-hour days of constant cross-training.
I'm tired of my drill sergeant screaming for fun.

It's exhausting to polish my boots every day.
It's exhausting to clean the entire barracks with a sock.
It's exhausting to fix my gig line every moment.
It's exhausting watching the clock, falling asleep full of thoughts.

There's countless instances I could be dreadful about.
When I signed up, this was not what I dreamt.
My recruiter said my training will be the best of the service.
But first I had to get through Boot Camp.

Tyrone Dicks

180 Degrees Of Subconscious Intuitions Around The Ocean & Moon: Feminine Frequencies

"Jagged Century"

Called to my duty as I stand watch over the horizon.
I see a village being pillaged, like Poseidon's fighting with Vikings.
My platoons armed at the ready, if they should come over acting trifling.
Were as one, worthy with glory, we won't back down, nor are we frightened.

It's a covert mission, like yesterday's reminiscence, as the days once past in a war zone.
Dispatch deployed to a foreign land full of foreigners, but not any one of us, will stand alone.
We stand strong like erections, with an air full of drones, meanwhile wanting to fall back and phone home.
Although, calling Tyrone, won't do us no wrong, we just want to be gone to where we once roamed.

I'm tired of the M.R.E.'s, and you can keep your S.O.B.'s, I'm just making enemies with endless artillery.
Also, it's hard to breathe, in this heat and fatigue and I'm tired of my sergeant depriving me of sleep.

And the morality of things contradicts my spirituality, I'm just done I give countless apologies.
But there's no remedy, until I finish my training streak for, I am a tired and worn out Jagged Century.

Tyrone Dicks

180 Degrees Of Subconscious Intuitions Around The Ocean & Moon: Feminine Frequencies

"Spiritual"

The Philosophy of Thought Process; abandoning overthinking for knowing, worry for peace, fear for confidence, ego for inner-attainment, physical for metaphysical. Freeing the mind to analyzed submerged facts and truths of the Universe with a bottom line of calibrating your frequency with the Essence of all Essences, in-the-now.

Tyrone Dicks

180 Degrees Of Subconscious Intuitions Around The Ocean & Moon: Feminine Frequencies

"Joyous (Hymn) Occasion"

(Repeat 2xs)

What a Joyous occasion...
I know my faults are my sins...
You don't need no Validation...
You are whom I depend...

What a Joyous occasion...
Won't let my heart get me down...
My past is just what it stands for...
I turned my frowns-up-side-down...

What a Joyous occasion...
I give my praises and glory...
To the One's that adore me...
They make me shine from within...

What a Joyous occasion...
For I tackled my problems...
With the Best Problem Solvers...
For with them I will win...

What a Joyous occasion ...
I know my ways are my own...
Although I strive for your likeness...

Tyrone Dicks

To live righteous fully-grown...

What a Joyous occasion....
Fight for my essence redeemed...
Because my faith goes the distance...
Greatness and blessing for me....

What a Joyous occasion...
I was lost now I'm found...
Blessed from my feet to my crown...
I'll make ya'll proud scream it loud.

What a Joyous occasion...

180 Degrees Of Subconscious Intuitions Around The Ocean & Moon: Feminine Frequencies

"What You May Not Know"

Reading is fun to mental.
Although it's now de-fun and dumbing down the mental.

The power of thought is tenacious.
As a mind is a terrible thing to waste.
You can do all things if you believe in yourself and be patient.
Combining them both and in time can make you great.

If you believe it, you can possibly achieve it.
Are words of wisdom, inspiration, and truth.
If Aborigines can read the minds of their own people.
You can do anything you think you could possibly do, you probably could read minds too.

Just know there will be entities and energies that surrounds you.
Because your high frequency would be a threat to their low vibration.
Some crystals, stones and meditation would help.
But a high vibration and focus, would be to devastate them.

Tyrone Dicks

180 Degrees Of Subconscious Intuitions Around The Ocean & Moon: Feminine Frequencies

"Speech Are Spells Worth Making"

Be careful what you say and how you ask for it.

Most of what you speak can be conjured to pass by speech.

Words are powerful as you can talk life into existence.

At any point in time, you can obtain, of what you never had indeed.

Spells are binding, so when you're spelling... be mindful.

I spaced It out, so it won't go over your head.

Grasp the depth of its sensuousness and over-stand the power it has.

And always, beware of what you've might have said.

Something thought to be so simple, of what we learned in school.

Could be something so crucial, later down the line within our lives.

Although, we go day to day not knowing the damage that can be made.

Or the greatness, that can come from how we strive.

Take heed to your speech of your everyday life.

As bless could mean to bleed within our being.

Tyrone Dicks

Although, speech is spells worth making.

So be mindful of what you're saying and take heed to what your teachers are teaching.

180 Degrees Of Subconscious Intuitions Around The Ocean & Moon: Feminine Frequencies

"Protected Connections"

Guarded by my Guardian, there's no fear of what I may face.

There's no pressure I can't withstand, no matter what has happened or will take place.

I'll devour what's on my plate, suggesting that I make no mistakes.

I'm protected through my faith, but I'm never not far from disgrace.

Draped in divine garments, that's connected within me.

I stand against the wickedness and bullies of bigotry.

Led by discernment, by faith and their envy.

Epiphany's my epitome, overwhelming till they send for me.

My protected connections have puzzled me in awe.

Blessed or punished, I struggle to respect their law.

At times I'm baffled, I can't set them apart.

Regardless of the outcome, for them I'll go hard.

I won't let anyone detour me or take me off my path.

I represent some of their traits, but I don't speak on their behalf.

No weapon formed against me, or chants not even crafts.

Shall ever prevail, so beware of their wrath.

Tyrone Dicks

Dedicated to reaching higher attainment, will be hard because I'm not without fault.

I'm not perfect, nor do I pursue habitual transgressions of sin, as I once was lost.

Although sin, can be a plethora of things, even though it won't stop me, win-lose or draw.

But, if I succumb to the dire temptations, that would be my mitigating downfall.

180 Degrees Of Subconscious Intuitions Around The Ocean & Moon: Feminine Frequencies

"And I Pray"

Unto the Most Honorable, the Most-High.
I Exalt your name and respect thee.
You're not only a blessing to my soul.
But, to my being you make me crave yé.

For anywhere I go and everywhere I be.
I shall not fear or falter, when I praise your essence.
You're not just my love, you're my teacher.
I pray you discontinue to chastise your pupil, with meaningful lessons.

My thoughts are natural, as they are pure.
They come with ease, as I freestyle my nightly tribute.
My inspiration by far on a night's eve.
There is no widow, for I am but minuet.

Whom wish to be Gigantic in this wondrous world.
This ever so revolving place, amongst this era.
As I've struggle, to maintain my beliefs.
I will not hold back, in the midst of Fear or Terror.

My gentle wind, I will be reborn again.
For whom you are extends, to the farthest reaches hence.
When my reformed commence, of the likeness that you deem-amend.
From all my broken promises depends on how I maneuver until the end.

My Grand Rising melody, my day light Salutations.
My High Noon delight, my afternoon Inspiration.
My midday admiration, my afternoon actions are blatant.
My evening Joyous occasion, makes my nightly communication.

Tyrone Dicks

More meaningful, when it's done in moderation.
Because there is no gratification, when I cram my thoughts to you all in one day.
I pick and choose when considering my speech wisely.
Because their favoritism of what I say and portray as I speak it into existence vibrantly.

You excite me, you have revived me.
Even though I thoroughly deprived thee,
You still let me breathe.

Let me do the most, cleanse the inside of me.
Let me be your Prodigy.
I'll forever magnify your name loud and proudly.
Please help me abundantly.

I am blessed to be loved from afar.
A star that mourned is whom you are.
For my ways wasn't pristine at all.
When I did my dirt after dark.

Never will I be perfect, never will I give up from trying.
Nor will I let my past hinder me, for what's ultimately mine.
But, in due time...
All my efforts will be sublime.

And I pray, this vessel, of whom you've created.
Much love.
Not yielding in undying, loyalty, and Dedication.

-Tyrone

180 Degrees Of Subconscious Intuitions Around The Ocean & Moon: Feminine Frequencies

"Undying Dedication"

I may fall, but I will get right back up.
When I'm focused on my objective, nothing will ever keep me down.
Regardless of the cards I'm dealt, I will be careful not to tarnish myself.
I must humble my core and meditate, before I receive my crown.

Before I obtain new heights, there will be a roll of the dice.
I will be tested beyond measure, pertaining to the weaknesses of my life.
There is no right or wrong responses; however, you act will set your path.
Be mindful of the ripple effect, because your actions may yield some pleasures or even some wrath.

Although, I often fall short when giving my daily salutations.
I try to make up for it with my actions along with meditation.
I'm not perfect, as I do most of everything in moderation.
They need no explanation, when I know I need to go harder with undying dedication.

Tyrone Dicks

Elevation awaits those who are true to themselves, and their core.

Even if I don't achieve my dreams and aspirations you must thrive on.

Being mindful and in-tune with the right frequency, spiritually can open doors.

Your thoughts are magical and could be conjured so live wild and strong.

180 Degrees Of Subconscious Intuitions Around The Ocean & Moon: Feminine Frequencies

"Harmonizing Chants and Prayers"

The title says it all for the jist of things.
Depending on the size of the mountain you want to move.
Put more energy, more effort, into your bigger dreams.
And all you may hope for could possibly come true.

Prayers in songs are more effective in general.
Like the hymns or prayers in Psalms for instance.
You have to visualize, harmonize, play it verbatim in your mind.
All your prayers must persist with commitments.

Strum your words like a lullaby.
As you should also, soothe your mind with your words.
Live in it every moment, it will come to pass faster.
Most importantly ensure your ways are preserved.

Because as quick as you receive it, it can be taken in the same token.
Either all at once or within layers.
Just to be cautious and be safe, ask for directions if you're lost.
And have faith when you're harmonizing chants and prayers.

Tyrone Dicks

180 Degrees Of Subconscious Intuitions Around The Ocean & Moon: Feminine Frequencies

"Greenery"

Inhale... The smooth sensation of open mindedness.
Exhale... All frustration of the day before it comes to a closure.
Inhale... Serene thoughts of beautiful moments of reminiscence.
Exhale... Slick remarks from those who gave you unwanted exposure.

Inhale... Mellow vibrations that sooth the inner being.
Exhale... Toxic energy that seeps into our pineal gland.
Inhale... Radiating nature, that exudes virtuous thinking.
Exhale... Negative notions, that holds on to some judgment of future plans.

Inhale... And take in all of your surroundings and where you once have roamed.
Exhale... figments of the imagination, that has no dealing with your current direction.
Inhale... sweet pheromones of the unknown and hold it in strong.
Exhale... Minuscule relations that tend to bring out your imperfections.

Tyrone Dicks

Inhale... The calm salutations of daybreak, if there isn't a child awake.

Exhale... The potent flavor of Greenery and enjoy the essence and of what it means to thee.

Inhale... The flickering synopsis of your photographic memory, brushing off what's at stake.

Exhale.... Relaxing your entire physical, while you enjoy and bask in all the scenery.

180 Degrees Of Subconscious Intuitions Around The Ocean & Moon: Feminine Frequencies

"My Inner Guidance"

My inner guidance...

Is so spiritual...

I'm feeling vibrant...

It's happening all my blessings.

I show my tithing...

In residual...

You keep me shinning...

The same old thing, keep investing.

My likeness...

Was minuscule...

You made me a wise man...

My ways have changed from learned lessons.

Forever vibin...

I can't get rid of you...

You can't deprive me...

There's no stressing, test and grace me.

My inner guidance...

Is so spiritual...

I'm feeling vibrant...

It's happening all my blessings.

Tyrone Dicks

180 Degrees Of Subconscious Intuitions Around The Ocean & Moon: Feminine Frequencies

"Dawn Of My New Awakening"

My spirits been dormant for decades.
My minds been cluttered for years.
My hearts been hurting for centuries to come.
And I'm tired of holding back the tears.

I humble myself when I meditate.
Seeking to explore abroad, astro-glide and explore.
I know I have a calling; it cannot be denied.
And I will not be overlooked or ignored.

I'm loyal when loyalty is given.
I respect when respected above all.
When I'm betrayed and crossed or neglected by fault...
To you, is whom I call.

You know my likeness, my ways and my passion.
You know I've been struggling to be alive lately.
I've been down but stayed strong and planning all along.
For the Dawn, of My New Awakening.

Tyrone Dicks

180 Degrees Of Subconscious Intuitions Around The Ocean & Moon: Feminine Frequencies

"Distress"

A feeling of *Anxiety or Depression* occurs when something is tough to cope with. It strains the physical and metaphysical.

Tyrone Dicks

180 Degrees Of Subconscious Intuitions Around The Ocean & Moon: Feminine Frequencies

"And It Hurts"

After all is said and done.
I'm the one that feel it the most.
I was the one who resembled the fool.
I wasn't the one who bragged and boast.

Karma is real, I know it to be true.
As the present is clear, brutal and painful.
Lies cut so deep, penetrating within.
No worries we all know, you're no Angel.

I got to stop from feeling this way it aches.
It hurts my essence of an anxious subconsciousness.
No more will I feel this way or be led astray.
And no one will continually feed me nonsense reflecting commitments.

After all I've done for you.
To think, you treated me like this.
I spent a few racks in a few months for who!?
Sometimes, I just want to say, this little B!+[#.

Sometimes it's true, that the good seldom finishes last.
I tried to give you what you said you never had.
Instead, you tried to finesse me out of my cash.
But you abused what you weren't used to, facts.

My efforts were worthless but was it worth it.
Was I not trying to give you everything you desire, I'm not perfect.
It's neither here nor there right now, this is our end, it's curtains.
I'm still hurting ... And it hurts... Shit!

Tyrone Dicks

180 Degrees Of Subconscious Intuitions Around The Ocean & Moon: Feminine Frequencies

"Facts, Or Fiction"

It's either facts or fiction, but my predictions are rare.
Some facts are hard to swallow, pretending to act like they don't even care.
Most fictions are obvious, and accepted by the masses.
Not caring whom it affects, even in the midst of calamity crashing.

You got to get in where you fit in.
Even if the shoe doesn't fit.
You make a way, out of none at all.
Or else, call it quits.

You get it, how you live it.
Especially coming from the trenches.
Soul ties can be so hindering.
So, I learned how to maneuver with pivots.

What's good for the goose.
Is also good for the gander.
Some lessons may be learned.
Other studies may be slandered.

It takes one to know one.
As birds of the same feather flocks together.
Being ridiculed by minuscule people is no fun.
Versus, despised by loved ones and being mocked forever.

I'm sorry but not sorry.
With no hidden agenda or point intended.
Has paved the way for mediocre insults.
As it states, you should never be offended.

What goes around comes around.
You shall reap what you sew.
Is the norm for all karma?

Tyrone Dicks

Ranging from all sides, to and Fro.

Rather it's a dream, fact or fiction.
Every side has a story to tell.
The moral, we can all live as one.
So, until next time I bid you farewell.

180 Degrees Of Subconscious Intuitions Around The Ocean & Moon: Feminine Frequencies

"It Hurt's So Good"

It hurts to find the one you love.
And they don't love you back.
The time you invested was a waste generally.
Now your mindset is thrown off track.

The moments you shared was memorable at the least.
Especially if they made your body feel so good.
You probably never experienced another freak so unique.
Not to mention, you'll probably do it all again if you could.

Just the thought of not finding another who can make me reach my peak, sexually.
Or compatible to my physical desires and all my needs.
Have me pulling at my hair, aggressively so to speak.
Because I felt, I already met the person of my dreams?

I might even try it again, because the sex was so nasty.
But it's times, when I don't even think I should.
A fetish I was addicted to, although she was a lot of bit fancy.
I was just uncertain, but I know the memories hurt so good.

Tyrone Dicks

180 Degrees Of Subconscious Intuitions Around The Ocean & Moon: Feminine Frequencies

"Jaded Intentions"

Misery on the horizon, if you think you're getting over on me.
Losses, there's no triumph if you're thinking closures coming.
I was lost alone and hurt; It was pathetic and such a shame.
When my eyes crossed and saw your eyes from afar, I must admit I didn't feel the same.

When I moved on you hated it.
But you knew we were separated.
Just to think, you played yourself.
Because thoughts of me made you devastated.

You might be pained without no gain, but in the warmest and worst way.
You left me drained from screaming your name; admitted I was heartbroken and lonely.

The times I've called.
You didn't hear me out.
You were nagging and yelling.
When I spoke you just got loud!

And after my downfall, you stayed with your doubts.
Knowing I gave you my all; It seems that you didn't care about...

Love comes twice around.
It's rare it comes a third.
I was lost, alone and hurt.
Even though I gave you all of my worth.

Tyrone Dicks

180 Degrees Of Subconscious Intuitions Around The Ocean & Moon: Feminine Frequencies

"No Love Lost"

All I wanted was to be closer, but, instead, I got some closure.
I really loved her; the allure of her decor gave me boners.
I had to detour, before she captured my heart again starting another chapter.
Bodied my heart, gaffled my soul, it's taking a toll that'll be the rapture.

I never knew a love like this, but was it the lust I missed?
Or was it her sensual kiss, or was it, the things she did?
Probably the sexual bliss, that had me turnt and all fucked up like this.
Or could it be all her stuff she gave me and gave nobody else, no love... In the beginning.

No new love found, and no old love lost.
I would've did it all and some, no matter whatever the cost.
She got my head all fucked up, pulling out my hair.
Writing all types of spoken words, but she says she didn't even care.

She makes me wanna grab her by her fuck'n neck!
Strip her naked, fold her up and put it all up in her chest!
But, ain't trip'n over spilled milk, it ain't my fault.
We separated over irrelevant shit, but... no love lost.

Tyrone Dicks

180 Degrees Of Subconscious Intuitions Around The Ocean & Moon: Feminine Frequencies

"Pain Of My Own"

To give a little and get a lot, is not what it seems.

That only happens in fairy tales, it's not what it's cracked up to be.

Wanting 50/50 but putting in put in 3.51 is a happily ever after in dreams.

And why I promote 80/20 regardless, because they always get more from me.

But these two women gave me more, without me even having to ask.

They always went above and beyond, and never made me settle for less.

Consistent in giving her all so freely, without knowing how hard the test.

When it came to sexual healing and fulfillment, they were by far, the best.

Not knowing what happened between us, then again back then I was cold.

Decades have passed, I lingered dormant but now I unsettled my mind to grow.

Now that I'm older and wiser, I can't wait until I see what the future may hold.

I may find two equivalent or better, regardless of kids, if there's chemistry we might elope.

They know my heart, my worth, my mindset; But they don't know me better than myself.

They know my story, snotty kid from the Jets; they know about the cards I was dealt with.

One day I'll find them, for richer or poorer: or sickness or better in health.

I'll commit to them all if they submit to my ways, because I know they're not corrupted by wealth.

Tyrone Dicks

"Real Mirages"

Some words have no weight to them.
Something like a ghost in appearance.
Especially from a bearer who deliberately misguide their speech to you.
A real trickster, don't trust them, this is coming from experience.

There's many that claim their real thorough breed's.
Making their power of persuasion seem beautiful.
Disguising mirages being capricious as can be at times.
Knowing that their feelings aren't really what's mutual.

Positioning themselves right up under you, playing ever so close to you.
Gathering any and all evidence and pertinent Intel.
So, they can fall back and plot and plan at the opportune time.
Then report back to their comrades with *a plot* to tell.

All of the skeletons that's in your closets.
Or, the secrets that was once hidden.
Will soon alter your direction and reality.
And position you in critical predicaments.

Be mindful of the shoulder you cry on.
It's rare to relate to one's losses.
Some energies may gas you up, to gain your trust.
Because there is a such thing called, Real Mirages.

Tyrone Dicks

180 Degrees Of Subconscious Intuitions Around The Ocean & Moon: Feminine Frequencies

"When It Rain It Pours"

Staring out the window as the water beats on the glass.

Thinking about the past when I was said to be her last.

Should've never confided in her astounding sexy ass!

I wrecked out and crashed, my emotional roller coaster wasn't gone pass.

All her tests, and all her games, so unapologetic, she saw me as a lame.

This dame came into my life and brought me both pleasure and pain.

Saying she'll change, instead her pretty little fangs, sucked and stroked my girthy long vein.

It was so strange, I could barely maintain, not knowing what a few months with that mouth would bring.

Blinded by her lust, all I wanted was to be with her and so-so rough.

My eyes wide shut, my inner thoughts was telling me to leave, I could feel it in my gut.

But, I was her duck, and it wasn't just my luck, and the things I did just to feel that nut…! Memories.

She did a lot of stuff, I was captivated and cuffed, saying she didn't want no other woman for me to fuck!

My heart was ripped and sore, yet I still write this letter staring at the door.

As my heart still adores, your touch, sentimental a midst this thunderstorm galore.

You've hurt me to my core, I may not see another the same, not now or no more.

Sincerely yours, DaddyBaby, drenched in tears, because when it rains it pours.

Tyrone Dicks

180 Degrees Of Subconscious Intuitions Around The Ocean & Moon: Feminine Frequencies

"The Abuse Must stop"

Drowning in disbelief.
Is making it hard to breathe.
How could the ones that you love.
Turn on you so fast so it seems.

The more you do for a person.
And the less you know about them.
Don't add up in no equation.
Just know that, so stop your frowning.

They're not sturdy in the way you live.
They abide by their own imaginations.
Like a figment of stereotypes.
The ones that's for you truly have patients.

Beware of the serenading from people can't hold they throat.
They talk about everybody; they can't hold no water they choke.

Spilling your intimate secrets, embellishing stones abroad.
Making themselves sound honorable, while tarnishing your name on Gawd.
They silhouette's maybe provoking, because sugar does look like salt.
My advice, trust your mindful judgment, because your heart can get you lost.

Some people have righteous tendencies, but most, just lie a lot.
Don't be quick to trust a stranger, without knowing them, could be your fault.
I lived and experienced all of my writings, experience comes with a cost.
Don't set yourself up for failure, however, the abuse-must-stop.

Tyrone Dicks

180 Degrees Of Subconscious Intuitions Around The Ocean & Moon: Feminine Frequencies

"Shine Above My Halo"

A born-again failure.
Knowing I'm prone to fuck up again.
But life without many chances.
Would mean to live with no thoughts to win.

I assert myself religiously.
Not arrogant nor will I pretend.
I call on The Powers that be for help.
Myself and their whom I depend.

Within My Spiritual guidance.
They can be truly called a friend.
It's hard to trust associates, colleagues, or lovers.
I've been betrayed even by kin.

Not saying I won't put faith in someone someday.
They will have to deeply move me within.
Or comprehend no hidden agendas afoot.
Or else be shown by spiritual omens.

I give without thoughts of receiving.
A kind heart is indeed my sin.
I'm a glutton for punishment at times, concerning helping others.
As I'm used again, again and again.

You're not just my friends you're my Favos.
A salute to my amended ways you commend.
You're the ones who put the shine above my halo.
I won't contend as vice versa you're the ones I defend.

Tyrone Dicks

180 Degrees Of Subconscious Intuitions Around The Ocean & Moon: Feminine Frequencies

"Seeking Solace"

Seeking solace for transgressions I've been through.
There were a lot of sacrifices I've made.
It's been a journey, but there's nothing I can't do.
I was preparing for the road that I paved.

For my offspring, my bloodline, my kinfolk.
All my actions are beyond being justified.
I went through hell, all alone just to give out more.
A LONG TIME… deep inside… I have cried.

Cuh lame, a black sheep because I didn't reflect their image.
Labeled me lazy, for ignoring favors, far beyond a slouch.
Because I wouldn't conform to their ways of doing things.
They doubted my efforts, so it was by nature I took other routes.

Now I seek solace for indiscretions to keep my mind at ease.
To the ungrateful, I've done all I can.
Most have been around half my life, so it seems.
But neither of them knows, just who it is, I am.

Tyrone Dicks

180 Degrees Of Subconscious Intuitions Around The Ocean & Moon: Feminine Frequencies

"My Flower Blooms"

Even though it hurts to breathe, I try to cope and seek.
Better solutions for me, to reunite with my purpose, my seed.
Knowing she was taken from me, twice-over wounded feelings.
The one whom birth her wronged me first, but denials an addiction indeed.

She'll know the truth in time, that the one who raised her is bitter and lying.
Her actions are relapsing of who she is defined.
I hope her ways don't rub off on your innocence abroad.
The other half of you, are features of me, my energy a far.

You know I love you and I know you feel it.
No one will dispute the uncanny resemblance.
But the situation critical, just know I'm coming.
Fatherhood...Know I never ran from it.

She hid you from me, so I took precautions.
Preparing your future, having to take some loses.
Never giving up, Failures Never My Option.
My persistent drive is forever-flawless.

You have my skill set, and my ways innately.
Inherited my ambition, and creative tastes.
You just need some guidance, and your father's training.
You will surpass me, you know your filled with greatness.

I would never leave you, and that's my oath.
I always had a plan, for you and me both.
I pray your mom's hatred, won't stunt your growth.
Because how she feels, can ruin all l have wrote.

And all I've accomplished, leaving you no alternative.
From a struggling lifestyle to a better life to live.

Tyrone Dicks

And when you get older, or you might realize it soon.

Her temper is poisonous, but your immune and I can't wait till my flower Blooms.

180 Degrees Of Subconscious Intuitions Around The Ocean & Moon: Feminine Frequencies

"Drained"

I'm on the brink of winning or losing it all.
Feeling exhausted from back-and-forth contingencies.
When I'm hurt with anguish, it seems like they applaud.
Although they smile in my face, I'm puzzled to the meaning.

Nonchalant to the woes, of me swimming upstream.
I fight back the tears that consumes me daily.
Wondering if their sentiments are genuine or flawed.
Contemplating would their integrity jeopardize my safety.

A turn coat for the currency, for a thoroughbred is priceless.
In what fashion can you weigh one's loyalty.
If you stand for nothing, you'll fall for anything.
I require the bare minimum of what I give, not asking for anyone to spoil me.

I find myself back where I started; me grieving from hardships.
Backsliding all the way down, to square one.
Should I respond with retaliation, or maneuver so blatant?
And let the end result affect them, that I have won.

Turn my cheek and my back in the likeness that they've given.
Always responding as a mirrored image of one's actions.
Being numb to their stares and not provoked by their words.
Standing firm for my respect with-holding compassion.

Brave heart to my core, for a coward I am not.
Is the Iliad of my life, nor will I ever change?
What was once detrimental to my being, would be forced without reasoning.
If I let their tirade manipulate me until I'm drained.

Tyrone Dicks

180 Degrees Of Subconscious Intuitions Around The Ocean & Moon: Feminine Frequencies

"Cheaters Quarrel"

Once a cheater is always a cheater.
Is not necessarily true.
But if you betray the hearts of one too many.
You may have a point to prove.

Your reputation may precede you at most.
Making it hard to gain someone's trust.
Because the ones you seek to obtain their love.
Will think you're there for lust.

Reveal no hidden agendas or give no suspicion to questionable motives.
Don't let your eyes wander careless or your multiplier be led astray.
Or have your companion second guessing or thinking nobody would notice.
Because your new love can be your only and last that could possibly fade away.

Don't be afraid, be honest and brave.
After all they might be your physical insecurities.
From past relationships reflecting a guilty subconscious.
They maybe a mirror of instances within your impurities.

Tyrone Dicks

180 Degrees Of Subconscious Intuitions Around The Ocean & Moon: Feminine Frequencies

"Hindered Bi Affection"

Her beauty makes me lose my train of thought when I'm focused.

When others approach her, I hold my composure.

As I tend to get a little rowdy.

She's a feisty woman and not my property.

But she could've been, and I know this.

But some facts will never change, because she's for everybody.

The love and lust that's in my heart, will be now and forever without regard.

As the attraction will be always and forever there, but the hurt has left me ever so scared.

In my mind I want her to depart.

I got a feeling; she'll always be in my thoughts.

Until I replace her with someone else who cares.

And someone that'll show me, they'll be there.

She's the epitome of my lustful nature.

By any means, in the bedroom I would degrade her.

And vice versa, we're one in the same, as I thirst for my own sexual cravings.

Always on my mind, when changing courses in any direction.

Tyrone Dicks

But, I'm uncertain as she's a fine wine and I love my tastings.

Shake it off, I will break this curse although I'm Hindered Bi Affection.

180 Degrees Of Subconscious Intuitions Around The Ocean & Moon: Feminine Frequencies

"Betrayed Bi Fundamentals"

I like to think at times, if you show love, you'll be loved".

Also, too-much is given much will be expected.

I thought the one I love was a blessing from above.

But I was bamboozled, I was lied to and neglected.

My first thought it could be karma from my past.

As turmoil was the theme with no gain.

I was repeatedly punished but it wasn't my last.

Because most of the past decade, I was emotionally pained.

I may give up on being committed with no sympathy.

Feeling that one person is no equal for my balance.

A lustful energy as my companion's chant, feel on me.

Sometimes I feel like, I'm monogamously challenged.

No longer hurt with the anguish of past decades.

Thinking: My sexual cravings are too much for one individual.

I drown my pain in desires of romantic escapades.

As I try to cope by being Betrayed Bi Fundamentals.

Tyrone Dicks

180 Degrees Of Subconscious Intuitions Around The Ocean & Moon: Feminine Frequencies

"Down On My Luck"

It's all on me, and in me they believe, I got to do better.

Some people O.M.G. and count me O.U.T. but, it's no pressure.

But now I see, all in my beliefs.

They'll flock my way when I'm on my winning streak.

I'm running down on all opponents, and no preference to their gender.

No matter if your friend or foe, a lover or pretender.

I'm coming for my crown, just keep looking down on this underdog.

Because I know you know it's my time now.

No regards to your envy, my wardrobe on smash, check out my posture.

Sharp like a tack, on point to the T, you know I'm from the gutter.

My caliber is unique, I stick to my dreams and nothing lesser.

Everything somewhat my way, because I am of who they speak.

No lies, I strive, through the pits of broken love.

A sucker for affection and I did it all because…

A Black Sheep yes indeed, once was gullible but not weak.

Nobody will keep me down; I refuse to see defeat.

My inhibitions, match my intentions, a new chapter.

My peoples be wishing, be like your kin and accept this bastard.

Tyrone Dicks

In me but see, the inner me will reign supreme.

My blood dirtied my name, so it's hard to respect from when I came.

Since birth; I spread much love with loyal remnants as a lender.

Of everything I had, I gave them, they still wanted pensions.

My friends know I'm official, even enemies know my tenures.

Should I care, would it be fair if now I'm coming up, when I was down on my luck.

"Black Sheep"

Selfless… I'm a jack of all trades but I'm helpless.
The way I am, they show no love but ain't staggering.
Ain't no pressure when I'm dealing with the prejudice.
I'm extravagant… and I'm prévalent.

Modified, my potential and I packaged it.
Five for three's, two for one's and I'm booming bih.
All the fiends, word of mouth, say it's excellent.
I'm not selfish… It ain't no bullshit.

If walls could talk, they'd unleash all my skeletons.
A lot of pain, a lot of tears, depression beveled in.
My demeanor, my anxiety, avoids the devilish.
I'm not ravaging… being celibate.

Black Sheep, within my chi and I rep it freely.
Pride aside, staying humble, part of my belief.
By my lonesome, how I vibe, stepping casually.
Sometimes they envy me… I'm not their pedigree.

The world, on my shoulders, but it's not relevant.
Sophisticated with my lingo although my educate.
Talking out their neck, is what I'm dealing with.
They know my name and worth, because it's beveled in.

Tyrone Dicks

180 Degrees Of Subconscious Intuitions Around The Ocean & Moon: Feminine Frequencies

"Love Me Not"

Love me or hate me, I will be me regardless.
Even if I sacrifice, would that suffice; you will still be scorned, broken and heartless.
The times we shared was times I cared, I gave you what passion entails.
You brushed it off, saying I'm so flawed, exclaiming you're waiting to exhale.

So, I fell back, trying to relax, between us both knowing the facts.
Keeping emotions intact, no harm in that, resulting it was all an act.
You were the premise, I was the punch line, got me thinking what was the plot.
It was all a movie, a fictional story-entitled: Damn, she loved me not.

Tyrone Dicks

180 Degrees Of Subconscious Intuitions Around The Ocean & Moon: Feminine Frequencies

"Sincerely Yours"

The years we had between us had well known meaningful situations.
And what came with it was a lot of traumatic stress.
There's no denying your demeanor and sexiness.
To that I had a fixation, so I tried to bless you the best I could, and I must confess.

My kind heart gave into forgiveness plenty of times, but I'll take the blame.
I can only fault myself for the cards I was dealt; I'm the reason my brain strained.
I was far gone in loving you.
To put hope in us I was too gullible.

Your feistiness aroused my rowdiness.
Reflecting my past, that was passionate bliss.
I reminisced I was arrogant and full of aggression.
There was no question of my blatant intent.

You awoke what was silenced.
You made me vibrant.
You was so defiant.
I tried to give you guidance.

Furthermore, I implored.
My heart grew sore.
You were what I adored.
And, I was sincerely yours.

Tyrone Dicks

180 Degrees Of Subconscious Intuitions Around The Ocean & Moon: Feminine Frequencies

"My Hearts Betrayal"

I believed in you, you said you believed in me.
We believed in us, even though it seems to be.
You wasn't meant for me, I gave my heart to thee.
You gave your lust for free, to any and everybody.

The way you let many of them beat.
You was meant for the streets.
You said you would never creep.
You're true lies on fleek.

Not living what you preach.
A jezebel beneath.
All those wicked ways on G.
When I thought other men envied.

How they were looking but it was simply.
Them reminiscing wet wet skeet skeet.
When I found out, I couldn't even breathe.
And just to think.

I never thought you would be the one to scheme.
It hurt so much, but I have to set myself free.
And away from the agony indeed.
You was what I thought I need... My Hearts Betrayal.

Tyrone Dicks

180 Degrees Of Subconscious Intuitions Around The Ocean & Moon: Feminine Frequencies

"Dry Love"

They say, blood is thicker than water but sometimes that water wash the grave off.
Although bloodlines don't make you family, it just means your related, that's law.
I had bloodlines that crossed me, most bloodlines always doubted me.
A few bloodlines that falsely accused me of being a coward-hardly.

I have bloodlines that used me, for any and everything on gawd.
Some bloodlines think I'm lame to the factual, but they so fake and flaw.
I give bloodlines enough rope, to hang themselves because.
Some bloodlines dragged my name through the mud from family members abroad.

I never once tried to use them, nor have I ever put dirt on their name.
I always looked up to them, but they never pictured me the same.
Never knew some was filled with envy playing the victim role, I felt the pain.
Alone was I in a family, with halfway love and where mockery still remains.

Hopefully It Will Change.

Tyrone Dicks

"Figure Of Speech"

There's nowhere to turn if your backed against the wall.

There's none to mourn too if you're given no one to call.

Could it be I fell off, could it be I turned soft.

I'm throw-ed off wondering, could this all be law.

Did the norm change of how this reality is govern?

Is it all the same, or am I clueless or stubborn.

Maybe it's all an illusion just a figure of speech.

It's not illegal to think yet, so please take heed and speak.

I dare you to dream.

Tyrone Dicks

180 Degrees Of Subconscious Intuitions Around The Ocean & Moon: Feminine Frequencies

"Either"

Belief that *a perfect world* exist. Underlining an obsession with perfection

Tyrone Dicks

180 Degrees Of Subconscious Intuitions Around The Ocean & Moon: Feminine Frequencies

"Beauty Vs Brawn"

Beauty is a disease that you inherit innately.

A heredity trait given through conception.

It evolves in the womb but can turn you ugly.

By the hosts interaction and of the fetus perception.

The carrier has an important responsibility to govern.

They must be aware of their atmosphere and surroundings.

They must have the will to abstain from peer pressure and not be stubborn.

If they give in it may take a toll on their offspring.

Brawn on the other hand is similar and hereditary.

It can be built from scratch or found within genetic enzymes.

They leave traces of your family's legacy within the jeans we carry.

As they can be manipulated throughout evolution over periods of time.

You may be born with a muscular structure or a lean physique.

Or born with a tendency to create one.

However, you see it, the sculpting of your body will make you indeed unique.

Your silhouette will be the epitome of serenades for fun.

Tyrone Dicks

Beauty VS Brawn is civilizations cornerstone.

As opposites attract and similar likeness would have a rivalry.

This could be false in some instances, but to each their own.

Although it's common they're attracted to each other concerning Brawn VS Beauty.

180 Degrees Of Subconscious Intuitions Around The Ocean & Moon: Feminine Frequencies

"Memorable Maneuvers"

I know you like my style and how I vibe with my profession.
The way I pull up on you and just bless you with no pressure.
Memorable maneuvers got you hooked, and you know I won't neglect you.
Because I flood you with affection and that takes away your stressor's.

And then I... console you when I hold you, just to show you.
That I... care for how you're feeling when you're emotional.
Because I... influence the rendition of your energy wave.
Vibrating on a frequency of pure focus so you'll elevate.

I put you on my level, now I'm In-tune with your mannerisms.
I like the way you giggle; I love the way your body moves.
Your presence provokes my thoughts, I want to seduce your body's rhythm.
I cater to your desires, like a man supposed to.

When it's all said and done, you'll remember my memorable performance.
Wanting me all for yourself because I ravaged your physicals.
Disrespect you in my arms but respect you as a woman.
With permission not conflicting that of our maneuvers are identical.

Tyrone Dicks

"If Looks Were Surreal"

If looks were surreal.
I would be captivated in awe.
My confidence is not arrogance.
As I am one with many flaws.

If looks were surreal.
I would strut and have my way.
My thoughts will be relevant.
From every road that I have paid.

If looks were surreal.
There would be slight pressure for what I obtain.
But without resistance, there will lye no challenge.
And without pain, there will be no gain.

If looks were surreal.
But there not and were not imaginary.
But if anything's possible and you truly believe.
Then we could all be living in a linear reality.

Tyrone Dicks

180 Degrees Of Subconscious Intuitions Around The Ocean & Moon: Feminine Frequencies

"Subliminal Messages"

I won't come at you sideways.
Pending the situation, I may come at you indirect.
I remember one occasion when we were up close and personal.
I displayed my affection, but you were so quick to reject.

You threw me off when you bat your eyes at me.
Some moments, I want to push up on you thinking it's cool.
Its many occasions, I feel your energy clasping to mine.
But under no circumstance, I don't want to be anyone's fool.

An enigma, I find myself sometimes having.
When it's concerning you, I'm baffled, should I keep up with my persistence.
Knowing that you know I got it bad for you and my efforts isn't lacking.
Makes me wonder, will I ever get a chance to show this gunsmith my fully extended.

Tyrone Dicks

180 Degrees Of Subconscious Intuitions Around The Ocean & Moon: Feminine Frequencies

"Edible Figments"

I miss the moments we shared together.
Memories are fading each day.
Losing myself within the letters I sent.
However, my mind and my spirit I must save.

I poured what was left out of my all into you.
On occasion, we had issues with trust.
With proof, you chose, I had a lot to lose.
But it's no use if your mind is already made up.

Not knowing, I tried and tried I was thorough.
I was loyal, and now I'm hurting inside.
Technicalities made you mad, but I respect your tomorrows.
I never wronged you, nor have I ever once lied.

It hurts at the least, but I can't miss you no more.
Concerning any currents or exs.
But the fact that you thought I could do you like that.
Makes me weary of us having second chances.

I'll deal with the pain or find a way to cope.
Knowing I'm not the only one with blemishes.
But my feelings are feeling so injured at the most.
Because its hard to find tasty edible figments.

Tyrone Dicks

180 Degrees Of Subconscious Intuitions Around The Ocean & Moon: Feminine Frequencies

"GraySweatPants85"

My dating website jargon is exclusive.
My social media banter can be conducive.
To my behavior, when my manhood is protrusive.
To the women of my liking, were congruent.

So, I rise to the occasion, when on standby.
To satisfy every command, as we both lye.
On plush bedding as your body craves what it won't deny.
My inner me, wants all of thee and to rearrange her insides.

Both our energies, colliding while she explores.
My name and some obscenities of what she endures.
We yearn, in unison she screams for more.
She's at her peak, gripping these sheets as I skeet skeet and roar!

Round two, although my quick start made her cum fast.
I rev her body with my piston, feeling her thighs clinch.
She wrapped her legs around my waist, just to feel my hemi engine.
I grip her face, with my palm, she don't know she's fucking with.

Fast motion, I'm focused and while stroking and thrusting her pelvis.
I position the back of her knees on my shoulders, as I stick and move into her careless.
Pulling her shoulders into me, she's not for everybody; nor will I share this.

Tyrone Dicks

Her physical convulses, I grip her assets, squeeze and sucking her juices as I'm not selfish.

Her limbs grow dormant as my physical firmness stiffens.
I lift and twist and turn, as she's bent into the perfect position.
I slap her dense cheeks, until she moans a few times before I put this stick in.
Then pull her hair and Power Fuck her until she climaxes again and again and again; I'm so relentless.

180 Degrees Of Subconscious Intuitions Around The Ocean & Moon: Feminine Frequencies

"Sweet Leggings58"

Her screen name says it all.
Or is it her users tag, Sweet Leggings58.
Saying, she's old school and first encounters, she won't give me her all.
Although, there's no exceptions, even if it's our second or third date.

I must wine and dine her, she wants to be treated like a lady.
Iterating there is no whore, under her blouse and pants.
She wants her doors opened and the tabs to be covered.
Before she gives me her body, she wants me to show her a courteous and generous young man.

She's not a gold digger, nor is she a beggar.
Just put in some time and your world will be bliss.
She'll let me ravage and have my way with her physical.
Adding she'll satisfy all my needs, and my ex, I'll never again miss.

She'll be submissive to my touch, and compliant to my demands.
And everywhere I go, when I take the lead, she will follow.
As long as I won't deprive her of her wants and her desires.
I'll suck and fuck her on command and all her needs I will devour.

There's no limits I won't make for my forever-ever if your worthy.
I'll be your sex slave and mastermind as your my sex slave and backbone till the end of days.
I'll encourage you when you're weak with insight as we are a team.
Vice versa should be the intentions of the reader, and what this poem synthetically craves.

Tyrone Dicks

180 Degrees Of Subconscious Intuitions Around The Ocean & Moon: Feminine Frequencies

"The Little Things"

First off, I would like to thank the Gods I gotcha.
When its said and done, you probably thought I forgot all about cha.
And I don't want to experience living this life completely without cha.
Knowing the back and forth hurt us both; oh, the things we did.

The semantics between us took a toll, it was such a shame.
Growing nonchalant demeanor's, playing this old dirty game.
We complement each other, I don't want to fathom the pain.
There's no question about how I make you feel, you know how it is.

My phenomenal women with a body built so sturdy.
I can't let another have it, devilish goddess you know I'm worthy.
We got to stop bickering my lady, we both well over thirty.
I can't help but reminisce about all the times that we shared.

Our time isn't done between us, and I can't help but hope.
Our subconscious was taking notes because we both don't want no smoke.
Besides our Gods, our kids our parents, we love each other the most.
Your place is here and by your side; I'll always be there.

Moving forward, I'll listen more and give you unyielding affection.
In return, let me lead us with my keen direction.
If there's a problem aside from us, we're covered by my spiritual protection.
My phenomenal women, sensible goddess, you're my planet and I'm your solar system.

Tyrone Dicks

180 Degrees Of Subconscious Intuitions Around The Ocean & Moon: Feminine Frequencies

"Rising To The Amazement"

Just the thought of her touch is arousing.

The smell of her scent gets me in the mood.

The sight of her silhouette is profound.

Just thinking, there could be no limit to what I would do.

A beautiful feeling is our outcomes.

As feisty and fearless is her name.

Her heart is what I chase knowing I can't outrun it.

But if I capture her essence, I won't be the same.

Tyrone Dicks

"Energy Speaks Volumes"

My energy radiates fluently.
You can see it thoroughly as it's potent.
You might get drunk off my wave intuitively.
I exude remnants of an exotic love potion.

If my words speaks in volumes.
Then my energy translates in fathoms.
My actions would be out of your league.
Perhaps Eve, can over-stand this Atom.

Or try to tame me at the least.
As long as she's always vibrating at her best.
If she's willing, I'll absorb and deplete.
As long as she's stable and not a hot mess.

Because her energy can attach and rub off on me.
Soul ties to those, as for the inexperienced.
There are different ways to not spread this chemistry.
But, the only one I know, is to be genuine.

Tyrone Dicks

180 Degrees Of Subconscious Intuitions Around The Ocean & Moon: Feminine Frequencies

"Aligned By The Nature Of things"

My adrenaline is so captivating.

You know there's no hesitating.
When I state my proclamation.

She's gone be so devastated.

No flabbergasting or exaggerating.

My ways are addicting she's fascinated.
So please don't feel alienated.

I'm somewhat, infatuated.

You know you need no validation.

Of who's irrelevant or soon to be.
Just close your eyes and breathe fresh air.

Lose yourself, then think of me.

Brighter days are on the way.

Don't consume yourself with their envy.
Or concern your feelings of their jealousy.

Just fall back and be free.

Tyrone Dicks

"Exotic Unicorns"

I'm so in love with you.
I've been feeling this too long.
I tried to keep my emotions intact.
Because I don't want to do you wrong.

My sentiments want to show and prove.
That I'm capable of love and care.
I know you never had a man of your own.
In your past they were always shared.

I will always be there to console your pain.
So, don't you ever think of being afraid.
You've been abused, you were used.
So, forgive me, but let me say.

My therapy and sincerity are what you need at the moment.
Give me that opportunity, I would hold you together so strong.
I know I can fix your broken pieces your made up of.
So, relax and let me scoop you and take you home.

Tyrone Dicks

180 Degrees Of Subconscious Intuitions Around The Ocean & Moon: Feminine Frequencies

"My Body's Algorithm"

At times my anatomy is a catastrophe.

It's something I have to live with.

Nonetheless, I'm a masterpiece.

My faults I won't conceal it.

I'll pivot my likeness.

If it's subject to gravitation.

I'm addictive and vibrant.

But, I don't want to leave you devastated.

I have issues, I accept them.

Without denial or arrogance.

I don't glorify my problems.

If you respect it, let's commence.

I want to rub on your essence.

Let me see your spirit move.

Don't be shy about your fetish.

Because I might be with it too.

I'm no prude or a troll.

Don't matter how you see yourself naked.

Tyrone Dicks

As long as you have a kind soul.

I don't discriminate against any races.

The Biology in all of me.

Is attracted to assertive symptoms.

That has a craving for me to teach.

My Body's Algorithm.

180 Degrees Of Subconscious Intuitions Around The Ocean & Moon: Feminine Frequencies

"Seducing Your Speech"

Each and every day, my love is the first I see when I awake.
Just to lay my gaze on defined beauty is a joy, let alone the embrace.
I'll make no mistake, not to arouse her anger, knowing my place.
It's to be her comforter, her conqueror, her loyal mate.

You are my dedication, and half of all that's in me is allocated.
To all the admiration that I give you-you know I'm not faking.
Sincerely showing it blatant, leaving you devastated.
Though the sentiments we make; there's nothing to replace it.

I put aside my pride, and vow to tell no lie.
I want it to be only you that I confide, most of the things you want I wouldn't deny.
She says, it's not enough just to live, but you truly make me feel alive.
I cried deep down inside, coming to the realization that you compliment my vibe.

You're my sonnet, I loved the longest.
And when I palm it, through your garments.
I sigh.

You like my wild aggression, and that I'm protective.
I fascinate you when I handle your adolescence.
You know my objective... And like that I'm receptive to your questions.
You fell in love with my perspective, saying it's the only way to live.

Tyrone Dicks

180 Degrees Of Subconscious Intuitions Around The Ocean & Moon: Feminine Frequencies

"In. Fact. Uation"

You have no idea of what I have in store.
For you and all your curves, I'll caress when I explore.

Your exotic features, your keen demeanor, your mannerisms, I'll adore.
I'll be your other man, you'll be in love again, I'll have you-have you stuttering, and wanting more.

I won't be negligent or say your feelings irrelevant.
Instead, I will proceed so affectionate, displaying my passion all in my etiquette.

When I rip off your garments, there's no need to be alarmed.
There will be no harm, I just want to get to the warmest.

It's my Word, that of all your ex's I will surpass.
As you could relive sexual fulfilling moments, through my breathe or a sudden gasp.

Tyrone Dicks

180 Degrees Of Subconscious Intuitions Around The Ocean & Moon: Feminine Frequencies

"Mutual Sentiments"

No matter your ethnic, size or denomination.
Pertaining to my future Queen to be.
I'll treat you as royalty just respect our conversations.
I only ask to be loved without fault, loyally.

I'll conform to your hopes, dreams, desires and wishes.
If you submit to the same, there's no room for pretenders.
As we please each other's nature, both mentally and explicitly.
As well as our beliefs, morals and agenda's.

Be truthful and direct, don't hide behind visages.
Because resentment can grow, if one of us gets crossed.
Above all, don't change what attracts us, that's law.
For losing what's destined, could be at a great loss.

Mutual Sentiment is ideal within my Misses.
Maybe fluent or mediocre in her years, and not lost nor corrupt.
That reminds, of what attracts me, and not false pretenses.
As were a dedication to each other, for thy love and thy lust.

Tyrone Dicks

180 Degrees Of Subconscious Intuitions Around The Ocean & Moon: Feminine Frequencies

"The Meaning of..."

I knew on sight, I'd probably give my life when I saw this girl.
I knew right then, in love she's in, she would be my world.
Events took place, of what I could not erase, and if I didn't hesitate.
We'd still be together, my love forever, but I couldn't own my mistake.

I hate you; I hate you, rang through my ears, and I knew right then.
She wanted no parts, spawned broken hearts, it was hard to be friends.
Her entourage just snarled and gawked whenever I walked by.
I couldn't find the courage to approach this person, I just broke down and cried.

No advice was given, if so I'd relive it and the things I'll say.
Would be conducive to my thoughts, although given my hearts contentment, I portrayed an Idle rage.
I bask in my pain, and sulked in my sorrow, I was a coward with no pride.
There was nothing near equivalent to the amount of regret I felt deep down inside.

She was my truth...
She kept a heart of steel...
She lusted for the way...
That I made her feel...

Tyrone Dicks

I always see some remnants of her....

In my thoughts, in my dreams...

I tried to unravel...

What, it really means.

180 Degrees Of Subconscious Intuitions Around The Ocean & Moon: Feminine Frequencies

"Serial Lovers"

I don't want to keep it on a Hush-Hush anymore.
Your attractive and I gravitate to it mi a more.
I don't like reconnaissance missions, nor will I spy on thee.
Revealing my incognito delivering you, my all of me.

Top secret operations, this predator will put on hold.
No hunting of thy prey, for my hidden tenure, I'll fold.
One's affection can't be misunderstood or concealed.
The desire for passion is radiating from my pours and will be revealed.

Dreaming of you passionately, forever yours will be my agenda.
Making it known, my pulse thrives for you, I want to be inside of you, and full of momentum.
Lured by your motives, finessed by your vibes, just wishing to remain in sync.
Serial lovers to casual partners, then eternal mates, no more will you be my sneaky link.

Tyrone Dicks

180 Degrees Of Subconscious Intuitions Around The Ocean & Moon: Feminine Frequencies

"Soul Ties"

We were introduced by Kinfolk.
I was captivated on sight... Especially, when she said you liked your throat choked.
Fantasizing about the way you would moan, and how you're acting so grown.
Made me almost exploded.

Our first encounter was of pure ecstasy.
Reminiscing about the day's past, when I couldn't wait until you were lying next to me.
Your body structure is superb, I almost left in you, my legacy.
Knowing that you may never have another that's of my pedigree.

You're like a sweet dessert, where I find delight.
When days are dark and gloomy, your my light that shines bright.
You're some of the fire within my eyes, that prompts my soul to ignite.

I don't know what it is about you, but when I'm around you, I just can't get right.

You bring me joy and inspiration, you're my muse as I'm truly inspired.
My phenomenal woman, the only one I adore and whom I admire.
We're connected as one, no matter if good or bad happens between us, or whatever transpires.
We'll make amends for that occasion, before the same night that we retire.

Tyrone Dicks

Before the evening of when we fall back, I will give you my undying devotion.
The unyielding nympho in me, that will put this all nighter, into motion.

At the end of the day, I aim to make you burst fireworks, from our lust explosion.
Then let you mount my expressions, grabbing my rein, as I slurp some of your love potion.

180 Degrees Of Subconscious Intuitions Around The Ocean & Moon: Feminine Frequencies

"Honorable Man"

Pure in heart whenever intentions are involved.
He indulges in logic, leaving others in awe.
His tone is direct, not aggressive or harsh.
Drama and semantics, he has no interest; that's law.

One's posture of defiance and behaviors unique.
With an attitude and style his adversaries can't withstand-they shriek.
Sophisticated are some features with insatiable and powerful beliefs.
He's not average, somewhat phenomenal, though an Honorable Man indeed.

He struts with dignity showing confidence in his stature.
Well gifted in the streets, as in the industry he too roam.
Magnificent as he's marveled, having a cultural universal vernacular.
Dishonesty, and no beliefs, he never would condone.

Intuitive, reliable, compassionate and understanding.
Are a few of his traits, he will display on command.
As well as consistent, spiritual and demanding.
He's not average, somewhat phenomenal though an Honorable Man.

Tyrone Dicks

180 Degrees Of Subconscious Intuitions Around The Ocean & Moon: Feminine Frequencies

"Every Man"

Every Man needs a Woman, who will stick by his side.
We may get weak when times are rough, but your our strength and our pride.
We may get even foolish, when we're hanging out with our friends.
But you're the one whom we depend on, our lifetime lover and forever our friend.

Although the way we met, it was hard for me to believe.
I listen to people say... it's the strange things, that leads to our destiny.
Relationships I never took serious... I was afraid I'll get hurt.
But you showed me I could release my heart, and confide in you all its worth.

Because being in love... was a concept I never knew.
Although I altered my ways, and decided to give my all to you.
I don't care about the chances I had to take, because it was a wonderful, wonderful feeling.
Even though I knew my pride was at stake, but I loved all of the meaningful feelings.

And it's essential that...
Every Man needs a Woman, who will stick by his side.
We may get weak when times are rough but you're our strength and our pride.

Tyrone Dicks

We may get even foolish, when we're hanging out with our friends. But you're the one whom we depend on, our lifetime lover and forever our friend.

180 Degrees Of Subconscious Intuitions Around The Ocean & Moon: Feminine Frequencies

"Shea Butter"

Refined like pimp finesse tactics.
My scent is so luxuriant and fresh.
Feeling so fine, like the finest of fabrics.
When enticed at her best, she's a hot mess.

Thick in appearance to the naked eye.
Pure but tainted by worldly substances.
She likes to be rubbed in between her inner thighs.
When it comes to my flesh, she's in love with it.

I see her throughout the day about every few hours.
It's something about her effect, I think I'm in love with her.
The times I want her the most, is when she steps right out the shower.
She's all natural and practical, she's my shea butter.

Tyrone Dicks

180 Degrees Of Subconscious Intuitions Around The Ocean & Moon: Feminine Frequencies

"Hem Of My Garments"

My demeanor is astounding.

And attractive towards extroverts.
Because this introvert is captivating.

And demands attention from pervs.

My aura exudes pheromones.

So potent to the touch.
It extracts essence from all sexes.

And in all directions, they'll lust.

It's known that opposites attract.

And they can't help or deny, what they feel inside.
My sign speaks of a passionate euphoric emblem.

Similar to the 8th numeral symbology but amplified.

Confessions of a pathological nymphomaniac sex god.

Who's infatuated with cunnilingus.
Those who resembles similar or parallel attributes.

I can't help but feel so envious.

I'm a Dominant sexual enigma.

Who's on the hunt for compatible creatures.
Someone that shares a similar likeness.

Regarding my extensive energy signature.

Tyrone Dicks

My fixation is not of this world or realm.

As my algorithm thirsts for your comments.
My being has a hint a masochism, as you'll be lured in.

If you so dare to touch a Hem of my Garment.

180 Degrees Of Subconscious Intuitions Around The Ocean & Moon: Feminine Frequencies

"Sexual Fulfillment"

They say love often at times, is found throughout the air.
I say love is a find and can be found through mutual stares.
I may be wrong, but stay prepared, they may be older, they may be peers.
Though my sentiments are quite clear, and the love you'll find will be oh so dear.

And the garments in which they wear will be provocative provoking tendencies.
You may be longing for gratification, yet-instead, you might just feel on thee.
All of me wants everything, obtainable features, for all my needs.
Tis my remedy, my inner me, hindering orgasmic eruptions will set me free.

To fondle your essence will be my creed, I'll obey your desires, but only if you conform.
Being each other's puppet, and sexual slave, anything we long for, will be our norm.
Don't be alarmed, my clinging nature is for your protection, you'll see you're far from harm.
Although my charm is warm, just so you know, your pretentious star is born.

I'll go the length and weather the storm, from hell and back I'll go the extra mile.

Tyrone Dicks

Just to see your smile your oohs and ahs, I yearn for your vows, you know my style.
Half on a child you know my sex is wild, after my performance, there's no bow.
But, now that you're plowed, and in awe like wow, wanting more, but only in front of crowds.

Wiping sweat from provoking brows, there's no escaping my grasp from this captivating feeling.
There's growth on what we're building, I'll mend your broken spirit, with an inner commitment.
I'm diligent with my extended, ain't no chillin, cum get this pressure on balcony's bent.
Deal with it, no witnesses for forensics, just yellow tape and sexual fulfillment.

180 Degrees Of Subconscious Intuitions Around The Ocean & Moon: Feminine Frequencies

"Angelic Being"

If my angel had a name.

It would be Angel A. Bivensly.

For her, I would never play no types of games.

As I would forever, treat her like royalty.

Unto her, I will give her unyielding loyalty.

And make way, for the ground she walks on.

I'll display my affection noticeably.

In high hopes, of one day I'll consider us one.

Angelic being, beautiful essence, you're a goddess is what you are.

Phenomenal in every way, and for you I would go hard.

So soft to the touch; oh, how I miss your sensual loving.

Your graceful in approach, and by far an astonishing woman.

I will treat her in ways I never treated anyone.

I would do more for her, going above and beyond.

I won't argue, assume or be inconsiderate.

I'll be her yes man, on occasion saying you won.

Respectable in every way.

Expressing my sentiments all so cordial.

Tyrone Dicks

Knowing she loves the way that I play.

Her ecstasy would be second nature, all so normal.

Only forceful within the bedroom.

Abiding by all my standards and morals.

In the streets, she's mannered and meek.

But in the sheets, she's disrespectful, arrogant and informal.

If I can ever find my angel that's meant for me.

I would court her, accordingly, giving her all of my unyielding loyalty.

And if my angel still doesn't have a name.

I would name her Angel A. Bivensly.

180 Degrees Of Subconscious Intuitions Around The Ocean & Moon: Feminine Frequencies

"All Of Me"

Often, I hear romance without finance is dead.
Is that an accident waiting to happen?
But, due to my performance, if you're not with the program.
You'll miss out on a lot of dedication and satisfaction.

Currency doesn't bond relationships together.
Even though I'm not a slouch, I make a decent wage on any given shift.
Loving their income isn't loving them, you love what they can do for you.
Besides, I'm a believer in spoiling my partner, I'll clutter them with affection and gifts.

Your welcomed to my mind, to my body and most of All of Me.
So, connected, no one should be able to pull us apart.
Other than each other, because I don't do hearsay-hearsay.
I deal with action and facts and it's factual you'll have access to the feelings of my heart.

A bond unbreakable, and it could all be obtainable.
No rent to owns, no payments for lease.
Fairy tales and happily ever afters are fragments of the imagination.
Until then, I'll give you none fiction and most of, All Of Me.

Tyrone Dicks

180 Degrees Of Subconscious Intuitions Around The Ocean & Moon: Feminine Frequencies

"Looking for Laaa"

Looking for laaa, in problematic places.
Lusting for love, in Lustful designated spaces.
Looking for lust, where love is always vacant.
Still looking for laaa.

Looking for laaa, when love is fictitious or borrowed.
Looking for lust, I think I'll find love tomorrow.
Looking for love, but instead all I find is sorrow.
Still looking for laaa.

Looking for laaa, when its broken and hope it will end.
Looking for love, but instead I found a friend.
Looking for lust, always losing, but I know I'll win.
Still looking for laaa.

Looking for laaa, in a world that grew so cold.
Looking for love, will I find it before I get so old.
Looking for lust, realizing its love, I must first show.
Still looking for laaa.

Tyrone Dicks

180 Degrees Of Subconscious Intuitions Around The Ocean & Moon: Feminine Frequencies

"Hot Mess"

She knows she's labeled a hot mess.
She's been through some trauma and neglect.
Concerning needs, she won't settle for less.
That's why we vibe, I understand her we connect.

From high school through college, she progressed
Whatever she does, she gives her best.
One on one conversations with her, there's no stress.
At times she's focused, is when she's nearly perfect.

If you're thinking about coming to her, come correct.
If there's an issue concerning anything just address.
Respectfully to receive desired effects.
Anything other... She's coming for your neck.

If you love her, it may behoove you to profess.
All your intentions and what's in-store just confess.
You never know, just for you, she might get wet.
So, grip her throat, grab her ass and suck her breast.

When she's head over heels, she'll protect.
Her best interest is you and her nest.
All in all, safeguard her mind and her flesh.
She's a loyal woman, but also know she's a hot mess.

Tyrone Dicks

180 Degrees Of Subconscious Intuitions Around The Ocean & Moon: Feminine Frequencies

"Unadulterated"

Beauty is a statement of fashion within.

Sexy is components you portray on exteriors.

It's carefully calculated although it depends.

On statistics calculated of perceptions irregular.

Love and lust are both admirations'.

Often mirrored by symptoms of desperation.

While being on a pinnacle, where hope is vacant.

Implicating true lies when intentions are escalating.

DOMinism is a culture, I display perfection in my trade.

All parties are in one accord, controlled by voluntary behavior.

SUBmission is touché, let me be your 'sex god' if I may.

Give in to my instruction and let me be your fleshes savior.

Relinquish your everything unto me, withhold no boundaries and no limitations.

I'll learn your fears from body language, conforming to your rhythm and specific needs.

There are levels upon levels of traumatic barriers, but learning you entirely I'll be fascinated.

Engulfed in your world as your consumed by mines, giving protection, affection and everything you seek.

Tyrone Dicks

You're my prey as I'm your predator.

I will feast on your meat, as I will eat and devour.

You're a ballad of teary eyes as I would be your sexual craving editor.

Reconstructing your structure by consumption and with me you will be inspired.

If your inner self is dormant or deceased.

I can revitalize, you would be active and alive.

Concerning your joy, nothing is beyond my reach.

If you're down, I will lift you and provide.

Your insides with inner attainment from my inner amazement.

Or in layman's, my energy will affect you with devastation.

As a contingency, I will open you and play with.

Your clit with my tongue and make you take it.

While I fondle and caress you in forbidden places.

Invading your nakedness in foreign spaces.

Making you gasp and moan in different languages.

I'll do what you desire, you just need to name it.

To experience me and my efficiency of intimacy.

Gravitate to your wishes and dreams.

Wanting to claim me, I'll be all yours ideally.

Besides our kids, parents and higher power, you'll have my everything.

180 Degrees Of Subconscious Intuitions Around The Ocean & Moon: Feminine Frequencies

"Love Isn't Loyal, But Lust..."

Which aspect of either of the two "L's", gives more trust without asking for it?
Wait... don't answer that.
Which of the aspects of the two "L's", unknowingly tell on themselves, for being so whore-ish?
This... is a fact.

First impressions or imperfections, duration are mere seconds.
It can last a lifetime and would rub you either way.
As second chances are rare and could be preferred.
But what you deal with plays a lot on how you were raised.

Don't be elusive, be fluent in objectives.
So, your partner can be aware of your preference.
Because you can be neglected by misguided perceptions.
Or be played by your own tactical methods.

Be truthful, be direct, be different.
Most of all, be transparent with your message.
Let no one, especially those wanting commitment.
And don't look for reasons, just to be a learned lesson.

Tyrone Dicks

180 Degrees Of Subconscious Intuitions Around The Ocean & Moon: Feminine Frequencies

"All That I Am"

I'm her sun and she's my moon.
The first person I see when I awake.
She brightens my day and gets me in the mood.
Could it be by chance or by fate.

I would go the distance introducing those who are kin to me.
If she stands firm for me and no other.
Us against the world keeping tabs on our frienemies.
She's my forever-ever and she knows that I love her.

I'm patiently awaiting until she reveals herself unto me.
My pursuits are redundant on repetitively being scammed.
I grow weary of impostors with lust craving as contingencies.
The one for me, will see I'll give her all that I am.

Tyrone Dicks

180 Degrees Of Subconscious Intuitions Around The Ocean & Moon: Feminine Frequencies

"Déjà Vu Rendezvous"

You know how I feel inside.

You're the only one I seek.

I push aside all my pride.

To spoil you, however you please.

You really make my inner being sing.

I just want to give you all of me.

When it comes to you, there's no one else.

Your beauty is all I see.

Throw aside your purse.

I'm taking off my shirt.

I want to consume your body.

Giving you all that I'm worth.

You make my cravings thirst.

So much, until it hurts.

It's hard to hold on to what I'm feeling.

You're about to make me burst.

Tyrone Dicks

You know what's at stake.

It seems I have a lot to prove.

Finding love is never too late.

Furthermore, I have a lot to lose.

180 Degrees Of Subconscious Intuitions Around The Ocean & Moon: Feminine Frequencies

"Phenomenal Women"

Rumors are flawed, non-consistent and always at a minimum.
Her energy shines bright, hardly dull or impaired.
She stands tall and strong in their midst and never fearing them.
That alone is something serious that they can't even bear.

Her appearance is astounding to say the least.
She goes in hard at every instant, giving it her all or nothing.
She's genuine in action as it resembles her speech.
She will always and forever be a Phenomenal Woman.

The way she maneuvers is of elegance, there's no room for envy or pride.
Her mannerism is graceful, down to her core, and her code of ethics.
If you're in need of a shoulder to cry on, she's someone you can confide.
Humbleness and loyalty is embedded deep within her genetics.

Not blinded by the Nay Sayers, her eyes are open to every waking moment.
If I'm troubled by any outcome, she won't hesitate, she'll come running.
She would lift my spirit and hold me down and kiss me when I'm morning.
She's a lovable creation, and will always and forever be a Beautiful, Phenomenal Woman.

Tyrone Dicks

180 Degrees Of Subconscious Intuitions Around The Ocean & Moon: Feminine Frequencies

"Grown Ups Only"

For the relaxed and casual of mature crowds.
Being overwhelmed with joy is a wonderful feeling.
It unlocks the channels in your soul and lets you explore openly.
If you're troubled, you may find peace if you're willing.

Free yourself from your past and what your use too.
You won't get younger and you have one life to live.
Everybody is not out to betray you.
If you have no luck, then it is what it is.

Whatever makes you happy, enjoy it and be subdued in it.
There's no reason to be single or lonely.
You may be hurt, you could be healed, again and again.
You'll never know if you don't try, for Grown Ups Only.

Tyrone Dicks

Interpretation Of Reflections:

Cause & Effect and Outside lookN In.

Tyrone Dicks

180 Degrees Of Subconscious Intuitions Around The Ocean & Moon: Feminine Frequencies

Your Palm is an illustrated treasure map of hieroglyphics. Understanding the symbology, within the thin and thick lines-can guide you towards the gems of inner-attainment. Having the letter "M" signifies, success and prosperity; and is made up of significant joining lines; i.e; Luck, Heart, Mind and Life Lines.

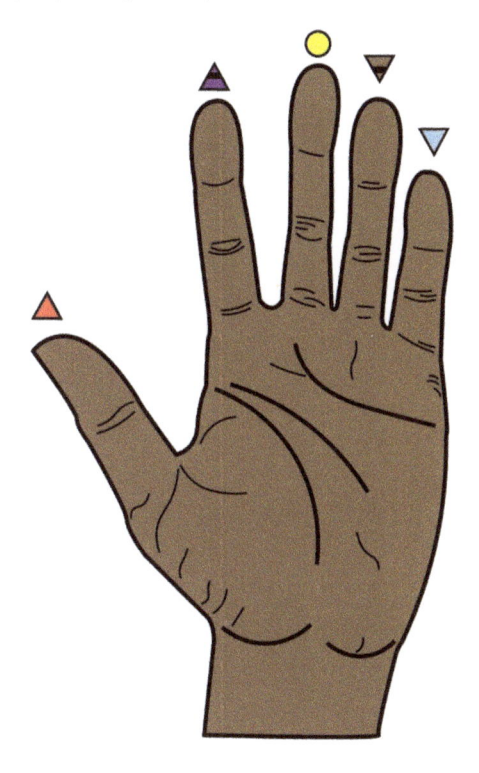

Don't be surprised that someone having a clear letter "M" in the palm of there hand is compassionate and helpful in their way of life. There knowledgeable and not easily angered. Although, procrastination could be there downfall. But when focused, there unstoppable with immediate results. There rational with critical thinking and will not venture into a situation without thoroughly thinking it through. Those who have the letter "M" in there palms, are destined for greatness.

Just know, the long winding road to get there will be inescapable. Because you are inevitable.

Tyrone Dicks

180 Degrees Of Subconscious Intuitions Around The Ocean & Moon: Feminine Frequencies

1. **Thought (Crown) Chakra** – Located at the Crown of the head. It strives on eitheric energy and is blocked by worldly attachments. Shadow work on what matters to you in this world. When unlocked, you will have ultimate consciousness and control of your premonitions and actions. Learn to let go and surrender yourself for Higher Attainment. *Letting go of what you cherish.*

2. **Light (3rd Eye) Chakra** – Located in the forehead. It strives on insight and is blocked by illusion. Shadow work and look with keen logic and realize the Biggest Illusion is the Separation of People. Were of different ethnics but of the same race. As there is balance without Illusion in the Animal Kingdom; there can also be in the Human Race. *Worldly possessions are enablers to the Intellectual.*

3. **Sound (Throat) Chakra** – Located in the Throat. It strives on trustworthiness and is blocked by fabrications. The lies we tell ourselves or other's, can eat at our souls. Denying who you are will halt great things from manifesting into your life. *Accept who you are, with all your faults, without remorse.*

4. **Heart Chakra** – Located in the chest. It strives on love and anguish. Shadow work on your sadness and loss of

loved ones. As they will be reborn back into your lives, resembling those we once missed. *Love for those loss, will always be there as they'll reincarnate back into our lives in someway, shape or form.*

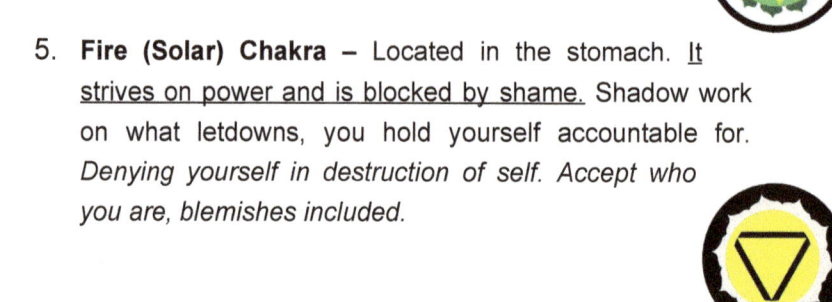

5. **Fire (Solar) Chakra** – Located in the stomach. It strives on power and is blocked by shame. Shadow work on what letdowns, you hold yourself accountable for. *Denying yourself in destruction of self. Accept who you are, blemishes included.*

6. **Water (Sacral) Chakra** – Located in the lower abdomen. It strives on pleeasure and is blocked by guilt. Shadow work on what you hold yourself responsible for. Accept what is and let it be. *Forgive yourself so you can continue to b a positive influence to others.*

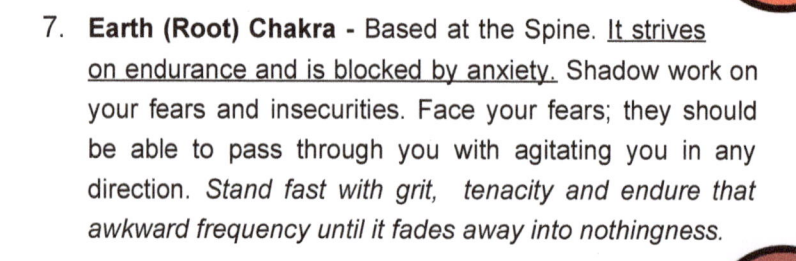

7. **Earth (Root) Chakra** - Based at the Spine. It strives on endurance and is blocked by anxiety. Shadow work on your fears and insecurities. Face your fears; they should be able to pass through you with agitating you in any direction. *Stand fast with grit, tenacity and endure that awkward frequency until it fades away into nothingness.*

About The Author

Born of a Beautiful & Strong-Single Mother in Urban Miami, Fl. USA. I had my occasional downfalls & set-backs as anyone. The growing pains in life was fun-yet dangerous. I spent most of my days in collegiate sports with friends and relatives. Or at home engulfed in a gaming console and/or bringing my Imagination to life; in different forms of Poetic Rhythms and Short Stories. I have discovered my passion for the Arts when I was 9, and at a critical stage in my life. Since then, I have entered countless Poetry contests in my adolescence; trained as a Broadcasting Tech. In Junior High. Graduated from MNW C/0 99 with countless accolades & files of intellectual creativity. I enlisted in the United States Navy for six years. Then I found myself trapped in the rat race not knowing what I really wanted. A dreamer as a kid, not realizing subconsciously back then; that I wanted to be a "Dreamer & Creator" as my Career Path. After 26 years of avoiding my passion, I finally gave in to it. Resulting me being happier than ever with my new direction. Now I am able to express my creativity with the masses of Entertainment, underlining Inner-Attainment. My Story, is just beginning and *this* maybe someone's road-map to inspiration.
Again, thanks for the purchase of my masterpiece.

www.IVPTME.com

Tyrone Dicks

180 Degrees Of Subconscious Intuitions Around The Ocean & Moon: Feminine Frequencies

Acknowledgements

First and Foremost, I would like to thank my *thought-process* for Never-Giving-Up on my Aspirations and Dreams; throughout all my sleepless nights, when other doubted the process.

Secondly, I want to thank my Beautiful Daughter Adely. The separation was Hard but, in time, you will realize what truly happened and *facts are revealed*. Everything I've done and doing is for you and your future. The thought of you give me the motivation I need to continue pushing towards my goals. I miss you so much... Always. We will be together again, soon coming.

Last but certainly not least, I would like to thank Dr. Vernessa Blackwell (www.chatwithdrvee.com) for allowing me to be apart of the 2023/24 Edition of "JOY 365 Devotional. Lamont Johnson for adding my color scheme to my illustrations.

This piece of literary work is amongst the first of several to be published.

A mind is indeed a terrible thing to waste, if it's not already wasted.
-Tyrone